EXPLORING EUROPE

Continents of the World
Geography Series

By
MICHAEL KRAMME, Ph.D.

COPYRIGHT © 2002 Mark Twain Media, Inc.

ISBN 1-58037-220-1

Printing No. CD-1566

Mark Twain Media, Inc., Publishers
Distributed by Carson-Dellosa Publishing Company, Inc.

Map Source: Mountain High Maps® Copyright © 1993 Digital Wisdom, Inc.

Table of Contents

The Continents

A continent is a large land-mass completely or mostly surrounded by water. Geographers list seven continents: North America, South America, Europe, Asia, Africa, Australia, and Antarctica. Greenland and the India-Pakistan area are sometimes referred to as "subcontinents." Madagascar and the Seychelles Islands are often called "microcontinents." The island groups in the Pacific Ocean are called "Oceania," but they are not considered a continent.

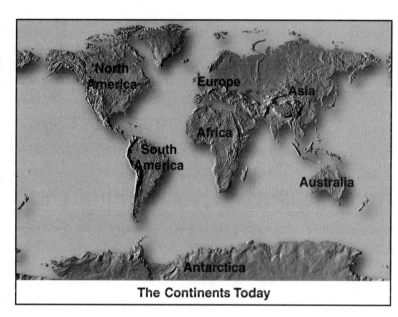

The Continents Today

The continents make up just over 29 percent of the earth's surface. They occupy about 57,100,000 square miles (148,000,000 sq. km). More than 65 percent of the land area is in the Northern Hemisphere.

HOW WERE THE CONTINENTS FORMED?

For many years, Europeans believed the continents were formed by a catastrophe or series of catastrophes, such as floods, earthquakes, and volcanoes. In 1596, a Dutch mapmaker, Abraham Ortelius, noted that the Americas' eastern coasts and the western coasts of Europe and Africa looked as if they fit together. He proposed that once they had been joined but later were torn apart.

Many years later, a German named Alfred Lothar Wegener published a book in which he explained his theory of the "**Continental Drift**." Wegener, like Ortelius, believed that the earth originally had one super continent. He named it **Pangaea** from the Greek word meaning "all lands." He believed that the large landmass was a lighter rock that floated on a heavier rock, like ice floats on water.

Wegener's theory stated that the landmasses were still moving at a rate of about one yard each century. Wegener believed that Pangaea existed in the Permian Age. Then Pangaea slowly divided into two continents, the upper part, **Laurasia**, and the lower, **Gondwanaland**, during the Triassic Age.

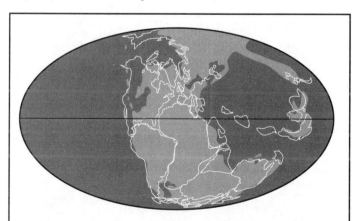

Wegener's theoretical continent, Pangaea, during the Permian Age (white outlines indicate current continents)

By the Jurassic Age, the land-masses had moved into what we could recognize as the seven continents, although they were still located near each other. Eventually, the continents "drifted" to their present locations.

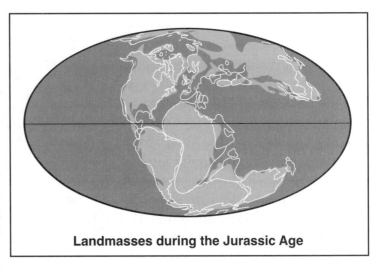

Landmasses during the Jurassic Age

Most scientists had been in agreement on the continental drift theory until researchers in the 1960s discovered several major mountain ranges on the ocean floor. These mountains suggested that the earth's crust consists of about 20 slabs or **plates**.

These discoveries led to a new theory, "**Plate Tectonics**," which has become more popular. This theory suggests that these plates move a few inches each year. In some places the plates are moving apart, while in others the plates are colliding or scraping against each other.

Scientists also discovered that most volcanoes and earthquakes occur along the boundaries of the various plates. They hope that further study will help them increase their understanding of Earth's story.

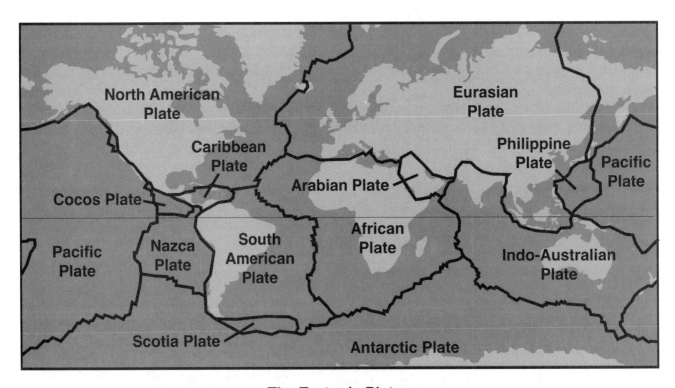

The Tectonic Plates

Name: _____ Date: _____

Questions for Consideration

1. What is a continent? _____

   _____

2. The continents make up what percentage of the earth's surface?

   _____

3. What was the name of Wegener's theory?

   _____

4. What is the name of the newer theory that replaced Wegener's?

   _____

5. What two natural happenings occur near the boundaries of the plates?

   _____

Map Project

On the map below, label all seven of the continents.

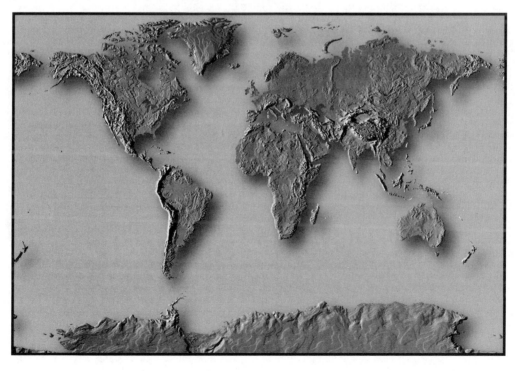

Name: _____ Date: _____

Outline Map of Europe

The Continent of Europe

Europe is one of the seven continents. It is actually part of the huge landmass of Eurasia. Most geographers agree that the border between Europe and Asia is the Ural Mountains, the Ural River, the Caspian Sea and the Caucasus Mountains.

Technically, Great Britain is not part of the continent. It consists of several islands. However, it and the islands of Crete, Iceland, Sardinia, and Sicily are usually considered to be part of Europe. The western part of Russia is included as part of Europe while the eastern area is part of Asia.

Europe is the second-smallest continent. Only Australia is smaller. However, it is the third-largest continent in population. Northern Europe is in the Arctic Circle and southern Europe borders on the Mediterranean Sea. The western coast of the continent is on the Atlantic Ocean, and the eastern border is the Ural Mountains in Russia.

Europe contains several peninsulas. Spain and Portugal form the Iberian Peninsula. Italy is a peninsula. The Scandinavian Peninsula includes Finland, Norway, and Sweden. The Jutland Peninsula includes Denmark.

Three of Europe's mountain ranges, the Carpathians, the Caucasus, and the Urals, are in Russia. Another European mountain range is the Alps, located in Switzerland, France, Austria, Germany, Italy, and Yugoslavia. The Pyrenees form the border between France and Spain, and the Dolomites are in Italy.

Europe's highest point is Mount Elbrus (18,510 ft. or 5,642 m) in the Caucasus Mountains of Russia. Its most famous mountain is Mount Blanc (15,771 ft. or 4,807 m) on the border between France and Italy. Its lowest point is at the Caspian Sea (92 ft. or 28 m below sea level).

In addition to its coasts on the Atlantic Ocean, Caspian Sea, and the Mediterranean Sea, Europe has borders on the Arctic Ocean, Baltic Sea, Black Sea, and the North Sea.

The Volga, in Russia, is Europe's longest river. It flows into the Caspian Sea. The Danube, Europe's second-longest river, flows into the Black Sea. The Rhone and Po flow into the Mediterranean Sea. The Elbe and Rhine enter the North Sea. The Loire and Seine flow into the Atlantic Ocean. Britain's most important river, the Thames, flows into the North Sea.

Europe has numerous lakes, especially in the mountain regions. Its largest freshwater lake is Lake Ladoga in Russia.

Name: _____ Date: _____

Questions for Consideration

1. What large country is located in both Europe and Asia?

   _____

2. What is the only continent smaller than Europe?

   _____

3. What is the name of the peninsula on which Spain and Portugal are located?

   _____

4. What is Europe's most famous mountain?

   _____

5. What is Europe's longest river?

   _____

Map Project

Using an atlas or globe and the outline map of Europe (located on page 4), label the following:

Bodies of Water:
Arctic Ocean
Atlantic Ocean
Black Sea
Caspian Sea
Mediterranean Sea
North Sea

Mountain Ranges:
Alps
Carpathians
Caucasus
Pyrenees
Urals

Peninsulas:
Iberian
Italian
Jutland
Scandinavian

DID YOU KNOW?

A lake is a body of water surrounded by land. Technically, the Caspian Sea, on the border between Europe and Asia, is a lake and not a sea. It is the world's largest lake.

Europe's Climate

Europe has two major climate zones. The western part of the continent has mild winters and cool summers. The southern region has mild, wet winters and hot, dry summers.

The Alps mountain range divides Europe into the two major climate zones.

The climate north of the Alps is influenced by warm, moist breezes from the Atlantic Ocean. These breezes help keep the climate moderate and provide precipitation throughout the year. This

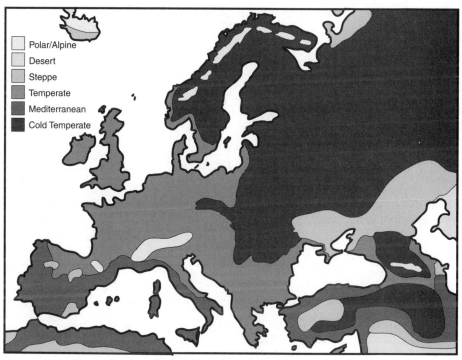

Europe's Climate Regions

Legend:
- Polar/Alpine
- Desert
- Steppe
- Temperate
- Mediterranean
- Cold Temperate

climate is sometimes referred to as the **marine west coast climate**. Europe has more of this type of climate than the rest of the continents combined.

The Alps mountain range blocks the ocean breezes from reaching the southern part of the continent. It also blocks the cold arctic winds coming from the north each winter. This creates a **Mediterranean climate** with warmer winters and hot, dry summers.

Greece, Italy, and Spain have a Mediterranean climate. Almost all of the rainfall in the Mediterranean climate occurs during winter.

From Poland eastward and north into southern Sweden and Finland, the climate is classified as **humid continental**. It is cooler and drier. This region does not have much of the warming and rain effects of the seas.

The northern parts of the continent also have cooler and drier conditions. The mountains of Norway block the ocean breezes, so much of eastern Norway, northern Sweden and all of Finland have **arctic climates**. Many of the mountains of Norway are ice-covered and have glaciers. These glaciers often empty into Norway's famous fjords. The northernmost regions of Norway and Finland have **polar climates** causing tundra soil conditions.

Europe has small regions of steppe, subtropical, and highland climates. Parts of Spain contain the **steppe climate**. These grassy regions were made famous as the location of Cervantes' book *Don Quixote*. A region of **subtropical climate** is in northern Italy and parts of Bosnia-Herzegovina, Croatia, and Slovenia. The Alpine regions of Austria, France, Germany, Italy, and Switzerland all have **highland climates**.

Most of Europe receives from 20 to 60 inches (508 to 1,524 mm) of precipitation each year.

Name: _____ Date: _____

Questions for Consideration

1. What is the main European climate type located north of the Alps?

_____

2. What is the main European climate type located south of the Alps?

_____

3. What is the climate type in eastern Poland and southern Sweden?

_____

4. What part of Europe contains steppe climate?

_____

5. What climate type is located in the Alpine region?

_____

DID YOU KNOW?

The Matterhorn is one of the most famous mountains in the Alps. It is a difficult mountain to climb. The first human climbed to its peak in 1865.

Climate Zones

Describe the following terms. Use a dictionary if you need help.

Tundra: _____

_____

Glacier: _____

_____

Fjord: _____

_____

Arctic Circle: _____

_____

Europe's Resources and Industries

Europe has a wide variety of industries and natural resources.

Agriculture is one of Europe's major industries. The continent is self-sufficient in most regions. Its farmers produce a variety of crops and animal products.

In western Europe, dairy and meat products dominate. In eastern Europe, crops become more important. In the Mediterranean regions, wheat, olives, grapes, and citrus fruits are the major crops. Other major European crops include barley, beans, corn, oats, potatoes, and rye. In addition to poultry products, herds of cattle, goats, pigs, and sheep are common throughout the continent.

Northern Europe, especially Sweden, Norway, Finland, and Russia, has a large forestry industry. Products include wood pulp for papermaking as well as lumber and other building products. Both Spain and Portugal produce a variety of cork products.

Fishing is important along all of Europe's coasts. Britain, Denmark, Norway, Poland, and Spain all have major fishing industries.

Mining has become less of a major industry in Europe than in the eighteenth and nineteenth centuries. However, large quantities of coal and iron ore are still mined there. Other minerals mined in Europe include bauxite, copper, manganese, nickel, and potash. Oil and natural gas have been part of southern Russia's economy for several years. In recent years, major fields of oil and natural gas have been developed in the North Sea region.

Europe was a leader in the development of manufacturing during the Industrial Revolution. Major production centers developed throughout Britain, Germany, France, Poland and the Ukraine. Metal products, textiles and clothing, ships, automobiles, and railroad equipment are still important industries. In recent years, Europe's chemical and electronic industries have increased greatly.

Europe has well-developed transportation systems. It has a major railway system, large fleets of merchant ships, and an extensive system of highways. Most countries have national airlines, and Europe's airports are among the world's busiest. The continent has many major seaports, as well as important inland rivers and canals.

Europe's governments created several organizations to improve trade, such as the European Union and the European Free Trade Association. On January 1, 2002, twelve European countries adopted the Euro as their common currency.

Name: _____ Date: _____

Questions for Consideration

1. What are the main agricultural products in western Europe?

    _____

2. Which European countries are noted for producing cork products?

    _____

3. What resources have been developed in the North Sea region?

    _____

4. When did Europe first become a leader in manufacturing?

    _____

5. What major currency began being used on January 1, 2002?

    _____

Matching

Match the following products with a country or region that produces them.

_____ 1. Citrus fruits	A. Denmark	
_____ 2. Cork	B. Finland	
_____ 3. Crops	C. Russia	
_____ 4. Dairy products	D. Spain	
_____ 5. Fishing	E. Eastern countries	
_____ 6. Forestry	F. Western countries	
_____ 7. Meat products	G. Mediterranean countries	
_____ 8. Natural gas		
_____ 9. Oil		
_____ 10. Olives		

DID YOU KNOW?

The Euro is the first common currency used in most of Europe since ancient Roman times.

Europe's Animal Life

Europe does not have the abundant varieties of animal life that it once did. Since humans have occupied so much of the continent for so long, many species of animals have become reduced in numbers or extinct.

Wild herds of deer, bear, elk, and wolves can only be found in far northern regions of Scandinavia and Russia.

Chamois (a small goat-like antelope) and ibex (a species of wild goat) are still found in the Pyrenees and Alps mountain ranges.

Herds of domesticated reindeer live in Lapland.

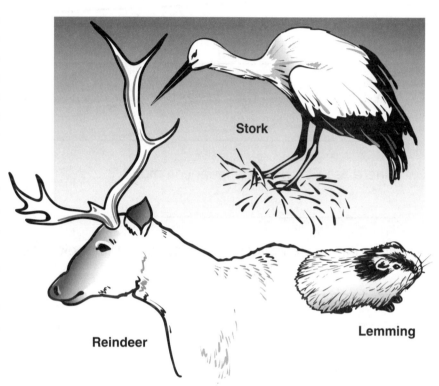

Stork

Lemming

Reindeer

Lapland includes Finland and the northern parts of Norway and Sweden. Reindeer provide both milk and meat. The Lapps once used reindeer hides to provide shelter. Reindeer are also used to pull sleds. They can cross arctic wastelands at about ten miles per hour.

Europe is still the home to several species of smaller animals. Ferrets, foxes, hares, lemmings, mice, rabbits, squirrels, and weasels are still found in large numbers.

Farmers throughout the continent raise domesticated animals, such as cattle, goats, sheep, and pigs. In addition to providing food and milk, herds of sheep provide wool for major textile industries. The British Isles are noted for their fine woolen products.

Several European nations have major poultry and dairy industries. Belgium, Denmark and France are noted for their fine cheeses.

Birds commonly found in Europe include eagles, falcons, finches, nightingales, owls, pigeons, sparrows, and thrushes. Pigeons are a source of food in many countries. Storks live in the Low Countries (Belgium, the Netherlands, and Luxembourg) and parts of Scandinavia. Many Europeans consider it a sign of good luck if a stork nests on their property. Swans live on many of Europe's rivers and lakes.

Europe's large fishing industry includes catches of cod, haddock, herring, and mackerel. Many varieties of salmon inhabit the rivers of the continent. Sturgeon live in the Black and Caspian Seas. Caviar comes from sturgeon. Portugal is one of the world's major providers of sardines.

Perhaps Europe's most famous animal is the legendary Loch Ness Monster. Its existence has never been proven. However, many people believe that it is a large sea creature that lives in Loch Ness, a lake in Scotland. The first reported sighting of the monster goes back as far as A.D. 565.

Name: _____ Date: _____

Questions for Consideration

1. What is a chamois?

    _____

2. What is an ibex?

    _____

3. Where are European reindeer common?

    _____

DID YOU KNOW?
Caviar is roe or fish eggs. Black caviar comes from sturgeon, and is often expensive. The more common red caviar comes from salmon.

4. What three European countries are noted for their cheeses?

    _____

5. What legendary monster may live in a lake in Scotland?

    _____

For Further Research

Choose one of the animals mentioned in the narrative with which you are less familiar. Use at least two sources to help you. Write a paragraph in the space below describing this animal.

_____

_____

_____

_____

_____

_____

_____

_____

The People of Europe

Archaeologists have found evidence of groups of humans living in what is now Europe over 6,000 years ago. It is believed that the earliest people of the region came from Asia. Most Europeans are descended from a common group called the Indo-European race.

However, geography divided these early people into separate groups for many years. These groups developed strong common cultures that later became the basis of national identities.

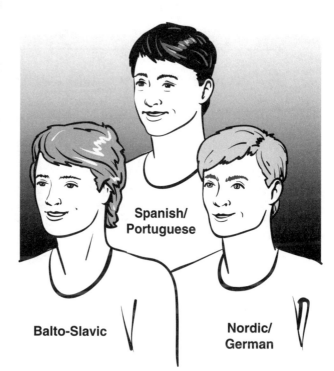

Even though these strong national identities emerged, some migration and intermixing of groups continued throughout history. Often these national groups became known as different ethnic groups.

Europe's population has remained steady for many years, and actually began declining by the year 2000. Throughout the twentieth century, migration from rural into urban areas increased. Europe has a larger density of population (people in an area of land) than any of the other continents. It has twice as many people as the United States.

Europe has about 50 languages. Most of these belong to the Indo-European language family. The Indo-European language family has three major branches: Balto-Slavic, Germanic, and Romantic.

Most people in eastern Europe speak Balto-Slavic languages. The Slavic-based languages include Russian, Czech, Slovak, Bulgarian, Polish, and Serbo-Croatian. Germanic-based languages spoken in northern nations include English, German, Dutch, Danish, Norwegian, Swedish, and Icelandic. Romantic-based languages of southern Europe include Italian, French, Spanish, Portuguese, and Romanian. Other Indo-European language branches include Greek, Albanian, Celtic, Gaelic, and Welsh. Many Europeans speak more than one language. English or French is the second language of many Europeans. Some nations have an official language and other minority languages.

The largest religious denomination in Europe is Roman Catholic. Protestant Christian faiths are concentrated in northern and central Europe. Other Orthodox Christian denominations are the third-largest group. There are Jewish communities throughout the continent. Albania and Turkey are predominately Muslim nations.

Most European nations have good educational systems and a high literacy rate. Many of the world's major universities are in Europe.

Europe is also noted for its fine health care services. It has the highest life expectancy of any continent.

13

Name: _____ Date: _____

Questions for Consideration

1. How long have humans lived in what is now Europe?

    _____

2. How many people live in Europe compared to the United States?

    _____

3. To what family do most European languages belong?

    _____

4. What is Europe's largest religious group?

    _____

5. How does the life expectancy in Europe compare to the other continents?

    _____

Matching

Match each of Europe's languages in the first column with the language family from which it was derived in the second column.

_____   1. Bulgarian   A. Balto-Slavic
_____   2. Danish
_____   3. Dutch   B. Germanic
_____   4. English
_____   5. French   C. Romantic
_____   6. Gaelic
_____   7. German   D. Other
_____   8. Greek
_____   9. Italian
_____ 10. Norwegian
_____ 11. Polish
_____ 12. Portuguese
_____ 13. Russian
_____ 14. Spanish
_____ 15. Swedish

DID YOU KNOW?

Switzerland has three official languages: French, German, and Italian.

The European Culture

Europe was the birthplace of what is known today as Western Civilization. The ancient civilizations, especially in Greece and Italy, have provided cultural inspiration for hundreds of years.

The architecture of the ancient times produced magnificent structures such as the Parthenon in Athens, Greece, and the Coliseum in Rome, Italy. In Medieval times, craftsmen built the great cathedrals with their Gothic arches and magnificent stained-glass windows.

Europe produced many of the world's greatest painters and sculptors. The Renaissance artists included Leonardo da Vinci, Raphael, and Michelangelo. Perhaps the world's most famous painting, the *Mona Lisa,* by da Vinci, hangs in one of the world's most famous museums, the Louvre. Painters such as Rembrandt, El Greco, Rubens, and Gainsborough were all European. During the nineteenth and twentieth centuries, Goya, Delacroix, Manet, Monet, Renoir, Degas, Cézanne, Picasso, Matisse, and Dali all made major influences on art.

Music was important in the ancient cultures, although today we are not sure of some of the details of how it might have sounded. The chants used in the churches in the Middle Ages are still sung today. The European Renaissance brought major changes to music. Opera was introduced in Italy and soon spread to the rest of Europe. A few of the important European composers include Monteverde, Vivaldi, Bach, Brahms, Handel, Hayden, Mozart, Beethoven, Schubert, Mendelssohn, Chopin, and Wagner. Europe continued to have important contributions to music in the twentieth century, including The Beatles.

Europe was home to a distinguished group of authors. The ancient Greek poet Homer wrote two of the world's classics, the *Iliad* and the *Odyssey.* The Greek philosopher Aristotle wrote the first major literary criticism, *The Poetics.* Other major European authors include France's Hugo and Dumas, Italy's Machiavelli, Germany's Goethe, Spain's Cervantes, Norway's Ibsen, England's Dickens, and Denmark's Hans Christian Andersen. The most important European author may have been William Shakespeare, whose plays are still performed more often each year than any other playwright, living or dead.

Dance has been an important part of the arts in Europe since ancient times. During the Renaissance, the ballet was developed in France. Later, the waltz was made famous in Vienna. Many European ethnic groups still perform traditional folk dances from their cultures.

Europe is still an important cultural center of the world. It is famous for many of its museums, theaters, opera houses, and galleries. European artists still have a major impact on world art.

Name: _____ Date: _____

Questions for Consideration

1. Who was Germany's most famous author?

   _____

2. What kind of music was popular in the Middle Ages?

   _____

3. Where was opera introduced?

   _____

4. Where was the waltz made famous?

   _____

5. Who is probably Europe's most famous author?

   _____

Matching

Match the terms in the right column with the most closely related term in the left column.

_____ 1. Chopin   A. Architecture

_____ 2. Cervantes   B. Literature

_____ 3. Cézanne   C. Music

_____ 4. Coliseum   D. Painting

_____ 5. *Iliad*

_____ 6. Manet

_____ 7. *Mona Lisa*

_____ 8. Parthenon

_____ 9. Rembrandt

_____ 10. Vivaldi

DID YOU KNOW?

Many of the major roads in Europe today follow the same roads made by the ancient Romans.

Scandinavia

Scandinavia is the name often used to indicate the countries of Northern Europe. It includes Denmark, Finland, Iceland, Norway, and Sweden.

The Scandinavian countries are mostly surrounded by water, including the Atlantic Ocean, North Sea, Baltic Sea, Norwegian Sea, and several gulfs. All of the countries have major fishing industries.

Denmark has the smallest area of land but the second-largest population of the Scandinavian countries. It also has the mildest climate and best soil. Denmark's exports include dairy products, meats, poultry, and eggs. Manufacturing is Denmark's largest industry. It imports many raw materials and exports finished products. Denmark's capital, Copenhagen, is the largest urban area in Scandinavia. Denmark is a parliamentary monarchy.

Finland was ruled by Denmark, Sweden, and Russia until it gained its independence in 1917. It is too cold and its soils are too poor to have a major agricultural industry. It does produce textiles and some metal products. Wood and wood products are its major industry. These provide over one-half of Finland's exports.

Iceland is an island and is not technically part of the continent of Europe; however, it is usually included as a European country. It is made of volcanic rock. Iceland is the westernmost part of Europe. It lies just south of the Arctic Circle. Most of Iceland's settlers came from Denmark and Norway. It continued to have political ties to Denmark until it became an independent republic. Less than two percent of its land is farmed. Over 80 percent of Iceland's exports are based on the fishing industry.

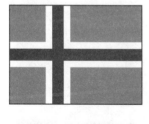

Norway gained its independence from Sweden in 1905. It is a constitutional monarchy. Norway is a mountainous country and has little land available for agriculture. It has one of the world's largest fishing industries. It produces significant amounts of hydroelectric power. Recent discoveries of petroleum and natural gas in Norway's offshore regions will have a major impact on its future economy.

Sweden has agricultural and dairy industries in its southern region. Forest and woodland cover over 60 percent of the country. Sweden also has large deposits of iron, copper, lead, manganese, and some gold and silver. It has several manufacturing plants noted for producing stainless steel, furniture, glassware, electronics, aircraft, and automobiles. Sweden is governed by a constitutional monarchy.

Name: _____ Date: _____

Questions for Consideration

1. What is the smallest Scandinavian nation?

   _____

2. What is the largest urban area in Scandinavia?

   _____

3. What provides over one-half of Finland's exports?

   _____

4. What Scandinavian nation is an island?

   _____

5. In which Scandinavian nation have petroleum and natural gas recently been discovered?

   _____

Map Project

On the map, label the following:

Denmark
Finland
Iceland
Norway
Sweden

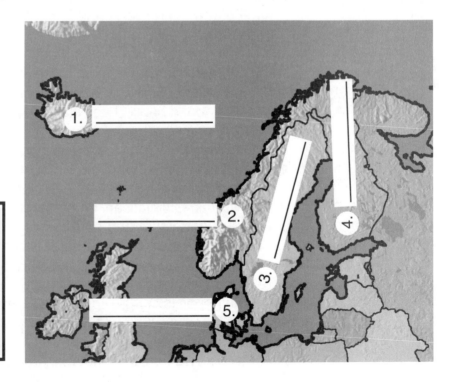

DID YOU KNOW?
Iceland is governed by the Althing. It is the world's oldest legislature.

The British Isles

Although the British Isles are not part of the continent of Europe, they are always included as part of Europe. The largest islands are Britain and Ireland. In addition, there are many smaller islands.

The British Isles have two major political units: the Republic of Ireland and the United Kingdom. The United Kingdom is often referred to as Great Britain. The major units of the United Kingdom (UK) are England, Scotland, Wales, and Northern Ireland.

Great Britain is governed by a democratic parliament but still retains a monarchy. Queen Elizabeth II celebrated her fiftieth anniversary as Britain's monarch in 2002.

London is the capital of the United Kingdom and is located on the Thames River. London's location has made it a major port and center of commerce for hundreds of years.

England became a major world power when its navy defeated the Spanish navy in 1588. During the Industrial Revolution, Great Britain became a major manufacturing center.

At one time, Great Britain had colonies located throughout the world. A famous saying for many years was that "the sun never sets on the British Empire." Great Britain controlled the American colonies until they gained independence in the Revolutionary War. After World War II, many other British colonies gained independence.

England occupies the largest part of the island of Britain. It is also the political, economic, and cultural center of the United Kingdom.

Scotland is located to the north of England and is noted for its highlands. Major Scottish industries include raising sheep, cattle, and horses. Large oil and gas reserves in the North Sea have helped to boost Scotland's economy.

Wales borders England on the west. It is known for its rugged landscape. It has large coal deposits. Wales' major industries include coal mining, fishing, and agriculture.

Northern Ireland is part of the United Kingdom rather than part of the Republic of Ireland. Northern Ireland remains in conflict and turmoil. Protestants of the region generally favor remaining part of the United Kingdom, while the Catholics generally favor becoming part of the Republic of Ireland.

The Republic of Ireland became recognized as separate from Great Britain in 1920 and as an independent nation in 1949. It occupies five-sixths of the island of Ireland. Dublin is its capital. Agriculture is the nation's leading industry. In addition to crops, the Irish raise sheep, beef cattle, and horses. Ireland also has important manufacturing centers.

Name: _____ Date: _____

Questions for Consideration

1. What are the two major political units of the British Isles?

    _____

2. What is the capital of the United Kingdom?

    _____

3. What unit of the UK borders on the west of England?

    _____

4. What part of the island of Ireland remains under British control?

    _____

5. In what year did the Republic of Ireland separate from Great Britain?

    _____

Map Project

On the map, label the following:

England   Northern Ireland
Scotland   Republic of Ireland
Wales   Atlantic Ocean
North Sea   English Channel

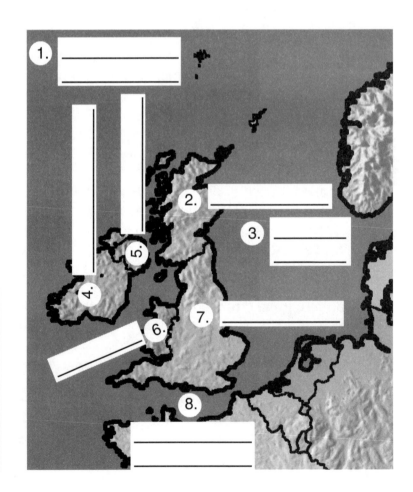

DID YOU KNOW?

In 1993, a tunnel connecting England and France opened. Known as "the chunnel," it is the world's longest underwater tunnel.

Southern Europe

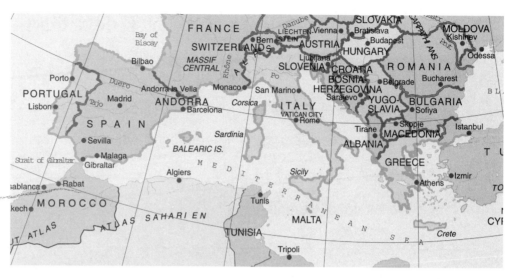

Southern Europe is often referred to as Mediterranean Europe. The countries of southern Europe include Greece, Italy, Portugal, and Spain. Except for Portugal, all the countries of the region border the Mediterranean Sea, and they all share the warm and dry Mediterranean climate.

All the southern European countries occupy peninsulas. Spain and Portugal are on the Iberian Peninsula. Both Italy and Greece occupy individual peninsulas.

Greece is mountainous and includes many islands. Crete is the largest of the Greek Islands; however, very little land is able to be farmed. Greek farmers raise wheat, corn, and cotton. Major exports include citrus fruits, figs, grapes, and olives. Athens is the capital of Greece and is also the center of its commercial and cultural industries. With its many ancient sites, Greece has a major tourist industry.

Italy is located on a peninsula that is shaped much like a boot. It also includes the large islands of Sardinia and Sicily. In ancient times, Rome, Italy's capital, was the center of Western Civilization. Italy is still a major force in Europe's culture and economy. Agriculture is a major industry in Italy, but manufacturing in the southern regions is increasing in importance. Grapes grown for winemaking, textiles, food processing, machinery manufacturing, and tourism are Italy's main industries.

Spain occupies most of the Iberian Peninsula. It is bordered by the Mediterranean Sea and the Atlantic Ocean. On the north, the Pyrenees Mountains separate it from France and the tiny country of Andorra. For years, Spain's major industry was agriculture. Wheat and barley are the major crops. Recently, however, manufacturing has surpassed agriculture in economic importance. Motor vehicles, textiles, paper, iron, and steel are major exports.

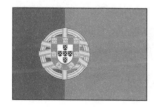

Portugal was once a major world power. Today, it is one of Europe's smallest and least-developed nations. It shares the Iberian Peninsula with Spain. Major crops are grains, olives, and potatoes. Winemaking, textiles, leather goods, cork products, and ceramics are Portugal's major industries.

Name: _____ Date: _____

Questions for Consideration

1. What are the two main aspects of the Mediterranean climate?

   _____

2. What is the name of the peninsula shared by Spain and Portugal?

   _____

3. What is the capital of Greece?

   _____

4. What is the capital of Italy?

   _____

5. What are Spain's major crops?

   _____

Map Project

DID YOU KNOW?

Portugal is the world's leader in cork production. Cork is taken from the bark of the cork oak tree.

On the map, label the following:

Atlantic Ocean   Mediterranean Sea   Portugal
Corsica   Sardinia   Greece
Sicily   Italy   Spain

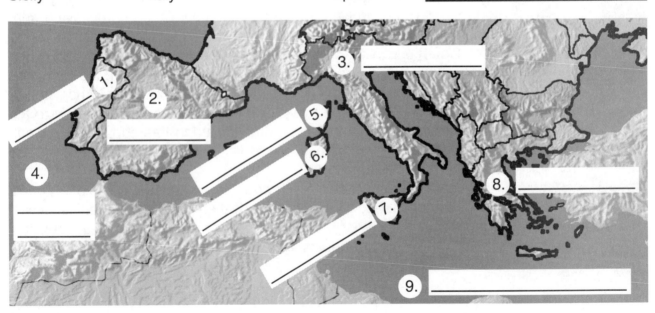

Eastern Europe

The nations of Eastern Europe are less developed than the rest of the continent. They tend to have stronger ties to the former Soviet Union than they do to the rest of Europe.

Albania is a mountainous country. It has emphasized its isolation and is almost self-sufficient. It is mostly an agricultural country. Major crops include wheat, corn, and potatoes. Large herds of sheep and cattle are also raised.

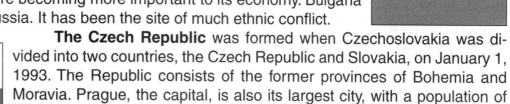

Bulgaria is mountainous and has few resources. It produces grains, fruit, and tobacco. Iron, steel, and textiles are becoming more important to its economy. Bulgaria is closely tied to Russia. It has been the site of much ethnic conflict.

The Czech Republic was formed when Czechoslovakia was divided into two countries, the Czech Republic and Slovakia, on January 1, 1993. The Republic consists of the former provinces of Bohemia and Moravia. Prague, the capital, is also its largest city, with a population of over one million. Major industries include engineering, agriculture, electronics, chemicals, iron, and steel.

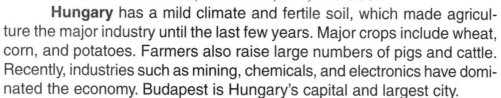

Hungary has a mild climate and fertile soil, which made agriculture the major industry until the last few years. Major crops include wheat, corn, and potatoes. Farmers also raise large numbers of pigs and cattle. Recently, industries such as mining, chemicals, and electronics have dominated the economy. Budapest is Hungary's capital and largest city.

Poland is one of the largest of the Eastern European countries. Its capital, Warsaw, is a major industrial center. Major industries include iron and steel, textiles, and machine manufacturing. Under communism, agriculture became less important to Poland's economy, but it has increased in importance in the last few years. Major crops include wheat, rye, potatoes, and dairy products. Poland's communist rule ended in 1989, and free elections were held in 1991.

Romania has a varied landscape. Its major industry is agriculture. Major crops include corn, grapes, sugar beets, and wheat. Oil, iron, and steel have recently become an important part of Romania's economy. Romania is the home of the legendary Count Dracula.

Slovakia had been a province of Czechoslovakia until the division of the country. It is smaller than the Czech Republic, and has less than half of the population. It also has much less industry than the Czech Republic. The Carpathian Mountains cover almost one-fourth of the nation.

Yugoslavia (Serbia and Montenegro) has many ethnic groups. Belgrade is its capital. Fruit, corn, wheat, and potatoes are its major crops. Recently, it has become more industrial, producing chemicals, textiles, and machinery. In 1991, the provinces of **Bosnia-Herzegovina**, **Croatia**, **Macedonia**, and **Slovenia** broke away from Yugoslavia to become independent countries.

Name: _____ Date: _____

Questions for Consideration

1. Tobacco is a major crop of which Eastern European country?

    _____

2. Prague is the capital of which country?

    _____

3. What is the capital of Poland?

    _____

4. What country, according to legend, was the home of Count Dracula?

    _____

5. What country had four former provinces become independent nations?

    _____

Map Project

On the map, label the following:

Albania	Bosnia-Herzegovina
Bulgaria	Croatia
Czech Republic	Hungary
Macedonia	Poland
Romania	Slovakia
Slovenia	Yugoslavia

DID YOU KNOW?

Hungary's capital, Budapest, was originally two cities, Buda on the west side of the Danube River and Pest on the east side.

Western Europe

Western Europe is noted for its major industrial and commercial centers and high standards of living. It is also famous for its great cities, which are cultural centers.

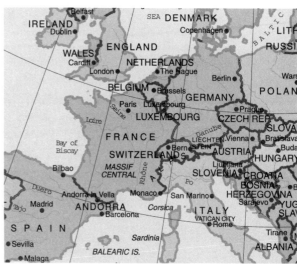

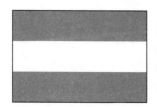
Austria has long been a link between the eastern and western parts of Europe. Both the Alps mountain range and the Danube River are part of the nation. Austria's capital, Vienna, has long been a cultural center. Tourism is one of its major industries.

Belgium is a highly industrialized nation. Major industries include metals, coal, textiles, and chemicals. It also is noted for fine pianos, cutlery, and chocolate. Agriculture is a small part of the economy, but Belgium is almost self-sufficient. It has two major ethnic groups: the Flemish in the north and the Walloons in the south.

France is the oldest and largest nation in Western Europe. It has borders on the Mediterranean Sea, Atlantic Ocean, English Channel, and the North Sea. Its capital, Paris, is one of the world's most important cities. France is highly industrialized. Major industries include high-quality automobiles, equipment, and textiles. It is also famous for its cheeses and wines.

Germany was not united as a country until 1871. It was divided into two countries after World War II and reunited in 1990. Western Germany has been a leading producer of quality manufactured goods. Steel, ships, vehicles, and machinery are major exports. Major agricultural products include grains, potatoes, sugar beets, and livestock.

Luxembourg contains only 965 square miles. It is densely populated and highly industrialized. It must rely on a great deal of trade. Steel has long been a major industry. Newer industries include rubber and chemical products. German is its major language, with French used for government affairs.

The Netherlands are famous for land reclaimed from the sea. More than 40 percent of the current land was at one time under the North Sea. Dikes were built and then the land behind the dikes was drained. Windmills were used to pump out the water. Cheese, flowers (especially tulips), and meat are major exports.

Switzerland is famous for its Alps. The mountains cover much of the country. The mountains and its land-locked location have helped Switzerland remain a neutral nation (avoiding war) through most of its history. It is noted for manufacturing fine precision equipment, especially electronics, cameras, and watches.

Name: _____ Date: _____

Questions for Consideration

1. What is the capital of France?

    _____

2. What Western European country is known for fine chocolate?

    _____

3. What country was united in 1871 and reunited in 1990?

    _____

4. What country is known for its land reclaimed from the sea?

    _____

5. What country has remained neutral through most of its history?

    _____

Map Project

On the map, label the following:

Austria
Belgium
France
Germany
Luxembourg
The Netherlands
Switzerland

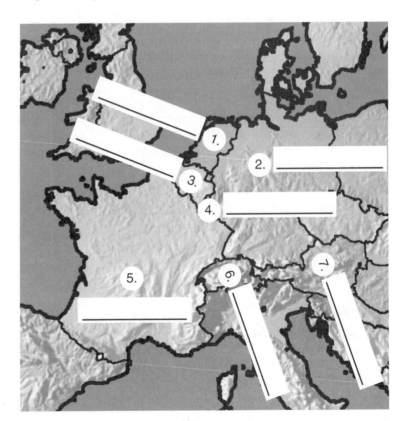

DID YOU KNOW?

Austria's capital, Vienna, is known as "the musical capital of the world." Composers Beethoven, Brahms, Hayden, Mozart, Schubert, and Strauss all lived and worked there.

Europe's Smallest Nations

Europe has six of the world's smallest nations. Each has less than 200 square miles.

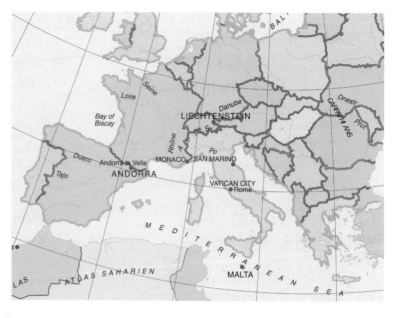

Andorra is 180 square miles (466 sq. km). It is located in the Pyrenees Mountains between France and Spain. It has a democratic government, but major decisions must be approved by agreement of the governments of France and Spain. Andorra's major industries include tourism and duty-free shopping.

Liechtenstein's 62 square miles (161 sq. km) is home to its population of 30,000. It is ruled by a prince, but he must have the parliament's approval of any legislation. Major parts of the economy include agriculture, commerce, and light industry. It maintains strong ties to Switzerland. Many companies have headquarters there because of low taxes.

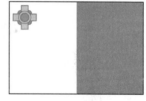

Malta is an island of 122 square miles (316 sq. km) in the middle of the Mediterranean Sea. It was controlled by the British for many years until its independence in 1964. It was a strategic port during World War II. Malta's major industries include commerce and shipbuilding. Tourism is now Malta's major industry.

Monaco has less than one square mile (2.59 sq. km) of land. It is on the coast of the Mediterranean Sea and is surrounded on three sides by France. It is noted for its mild climate and beautiful scenery. Monaco has no agriculture, and tourism is its major industry. Monaco gained international attention in 1956 when its prince married Grace Kelly, an American film star.

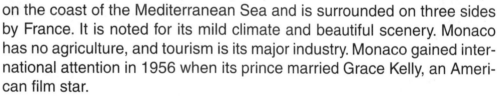

San Marino is a nation of 24 square miles (62 sq. km). It is completely surrounded by Italy. The Pope granted it independence in 1631. When Italy was united as a single country, San Marino retained its independence. Agriculture and light industry provide most of the nation's employment. Today, tourism and the sale of its attractive stamps and coins are a major industry.

The Vatican, also referred to as Vatican City and the Holy See, is the smallest independent state in the world. It covers just over 100 acres (40 hectares). It is the home of the pope and the center of the Roman Catholic Church. The major sites in The Vatican are St. Peter's Basilica, the Sistine Chapel, and the residence of the pope.

Answer Keys

The Continents (page 3)
1. A large landmass completely or mostly surrounded by water
2. Just over 29 percent
3. Continental Drift
4. Plate Tectonics
5. Volcanoes and earthquakes

Map Project (page 3)
Teacher check map. Use map on page 1 as a guide.

The Continent of Europe (page 6)
1. Russia
2. Australia
3. Iberia (Iberian)
4. Mount Blanc
5. Volga

Map Project (page 6)
Teacher check map. Use map on page 5 as a guide.

Europe's Climate (page 8)
1. Marine west coast
2. Mediterranean
3. Humid continental
4. Spain
5. Highland

Climate Zones (page 8)
Answers may vary.
1. Permanently frozen subsoil
2. A large body of moving ice
3. A narrow inlet of the sea between cliffs
4. A latitude that is about 66° north of the equator

Europe's Resources and Industries (page 10)
1. Dairy and meat
2. Spain and Portugal
3. Oil and natural gas
4. During the Industrial Revolution
5. Euro

Matching (page 10)
1. G   2. D   3. E   4. F
5. A, D   6. B, C   7. F   8. C
9. C   10. G

Europe's Animal Life (page 12)
1. A small goat-like antelope
2. A species of wild goat
3. Lapland (Finland, Norway, Sweden)
4. Belgium, Denmark, and France
5. The Loch Ness Monster

The People of Europe (page 14)
1. Over 6,000 years
2. Twice as many
3. Indo-European
4. Roman Catholic
5. It is higher than any other.

Matching (page 14)
1. A   2. B   3. B   4. B
5. C   6. D   7. B   8. D
9. C   10. B   11. A   12. C
13. A   14. C   15. B

The European Culture (page 16)
1. Goethe
2. Chant
3. Italy
4. Vienna
5. Shakespeare

Matching (page 16)

1. C	2. B	3. D	4. A
5. B	6. D	7. D	8. A
9. D	10. C		

Scandinavia (page 18)

1. Denmark
2. Copenhagen
3. Wood and wood products
4. Iceland
5. Norway

Map Project (page 18)

1. Iceland
2. Norway
3. Sweden
4. Finland
5. Denmark

The British Isles (page 20)

1. The Republic of Ireland and the United Kingdom
2. London
3. Wales
4. Northern Ireland
5. 1920

The Map Project (page 20)

1. Atlantic Ocean	5. Northern Ireland
2. Scotland	6. Wales
3. North Sea	7. England
4. Republic of Ireland	8. English Channel

Southern Europe (page 22)

1. Warm and dry
2. Iberia (Iberian)
3. Athens
4. Rome
5. Wheat and barley

The Map Project (page 22)

1. Portugal	6. Sardinia
2. Spain	7. Sicily
3. Italy	8. Greece
4. Atlantic Ocean	9. Mediterranean Sea
5. Corsica	

Eastern Europe (page 24)

1. Bulgaria
2. Czech Republic
3. Warsaw
4. Romania
5. Yugoslavia

The Map Project (page 24)

1. Poland	8. Bosnia-Herzegovina
2. Czech Republic	9. Yugoslavia
3. Slovakia	10. Bulgaria
4. Hungary	11. Macedonia
5. Slovenia	12. Albania
6. Romania	
7. Croatia	

Western Europe (page 26)

1. Paris
2. Belgium
3. Germany
4. The Netherlands
5. Switzerland

The Map Project (page 26)

1. The Netherlands	5. France
2. Germany	6. Switzerland
3. Belgium	7. Austria
4. Luxembourg	

Bibliography

General Topics:

Bramwell, Martyn. *Europe.* Lerner Publishing Group, 2000, 48 p.

Dunnan, Nancy. *One Europe.* Houghton Mifflin Co., 1992, 64 p.

Lyttle, Richard. *Land Beyond the River: Europe in the Age of Migration.* Atheneum Pubs., 1986, 175 p.

McLeish, Ewan. *Europe.* Raintree Steck-Vaughn, 1997, 48 p.

Porter, Malcom and Keith Lye. *Europe.* Raintree Steck-Vaughn, 2001, 48 p.

Sayre, April. *Europe.* Twenty-First Century Books, Inc., 1998, 64 p.

Treays, Rebecca. *Book of Europe.* Educational Development Corp., 1994, 64 p.

Specific Countries:

Cultures of the World (Series published by Benchmark Books.) Each book was published between 1994 and 2001, contains 128 pages. Countries included: *Austria, Belgium, Britain, Czech Republic, Denmark, Finland, France, Germany, Greece, Iceland, Ireland, Italy, Luxembourg, Netherlands, Norway, Poland, Portugal, Romania, Russia, Scotland, Spain, Sweden, Switzerland,* and *Wales.*

Major World Nations (Series published by Chelsea House.) Each book was published between 1997 and 2001, contains 32 to 94 pages. Countries included: *Austria, Belgium, Bulgaria, Denmark, England, Finland, France, Germany, Greece, Hungary, Ireland, Italy, Netherlands, Northern Ireland, Norway, Poland, Portugal, Romania, Russia, Scotland, Spain, Sweden,* and *Switzerland.*

A True Book (Series published by Children's Press.) Each book was published between 1999 and 2002, contains 44 to 48 pages. Countries included: *France, Greece, Ireland, Italy, Scotland, Spain,* and *Switzerland.*